RACE CAR LEGENDS

CHELSEA HOUSE PUBLISHERS

RACE CAR LEGENDS

JEREMY MAYFIELD

Mike Bonner

CHELSEA HOUSE PUBLISHERS
Philadelphia

Frontis: *At 30 years old, race car driver Jeremy Mayfield is already a NASCAR Winston Cup veteran with expectations of winning the grand championship.*

Produced by
21st Century Publishing and Communications, Inc.
New York, New York
http://www.21cpc.com

CHELSEA HOUSE PUBLISHERS

Editor in Chief: Stephen Reginald
Managing Editor: James D. Gallagher
Production Manager: Pamela Loos
Art Director: Sara Davis
Director of Photography: Judy L. Hasday
Senior Production Editor: LeeAnne Gelletly
Publishing Coordinator: James McAvoy
Assistant Editor: Anne Hill
Cover Illustration & Design: Keith Trego

Front Cover Photo: AP Photos/Chuck Burton
Back Cover Photos: AP Photos/Toby Talbot & AP Photos/Chuck Burton

The Chelsea House World Wide Website address is
http://www.chelseahouse.com

First Printing

1 3 5 7 9 8 6 4 2

Library of Congress Cataloging-in-Publication Data

Bonner, Mike, 1951–
  Jeremy Mayfield / by Mike Bonner.
    64 p.   cm.—(Race car legends)
  Includes bibliographical references (p.62) and index.
  Summary: Describes the racing career of the driver who won the Automobile Racing Club of America's Rookie of the Year title in 1993 and raced in his first Winston Cup race that same year.
    ISBN 0-7910-5412-8 (hc)
    1. Mayfield, Jeremy, 1969–   —Juvenile literature. 2. Automobile racing drivers—United States—Biography—Juvenile literature. [1. Mayfield, Jeremy, 1969–   . 2. Automobile racing drivers. 3. Stock car racing.] I. Title. II. Series.
GV1032.M24B66 1999
796.72'092—dc21
[B]   99-23254
                                                                        CIP
                                                                         AC

CONTENTS

VICTORY LANE
AT POCONO

Jeremy Mayfield gripped the steering wheel of his Number 12 Ford Taurus Mobil 1 stock car. Thundering down the straightaway at the 1998 Pocono 500 in Long Pond, Pennsylvania, Mayfield kept to a steady pace. He knew from past experience that the big front stretch at the 2.5-mile track was exceptionally tough on engines. He also knew that he needed to drive his Taurus perfectly to win the race.

The roar of the Taurus's high-performance engine drowned out the sounds of the other cars on the track. The loud noise shut out practically every thing but Mayfield's single-minded desire to win the race, for himself and his team.

Racing fans knew that the blond, crew-cut, 28-year-old Mayfield would make a last grab for the lead. Since the 1998 racing season began, Mayfield had crept up in the National Association for Stock Car Auto Racing (NASCAR) Winston Cup

A triumphant Jeremy Mayfield waves a towel in celebrating his win at the Pocono 500 in June 1998. For Mayfield, edging out his rival Jeff Gordon to win his first Winston Cup race was the fulfillment of a cherished dream—to be at the top in the world of stock car racing.

rankings, until he reached the number-one spot. Mayfield had not yet won a big race, however. He had come close to winning several times without quite making it. In two of the past three years it was Chevy driver Jeff Gordon, not Jeremy Mayfield, who had won most of the big races. Up to Pocono, bad luck had dogged every step Mayfield took.

At the TranSouth 400 in Darlington, South Carolina, Mayfield was leading with 43 laps to go. A caution flag let all the other contenders drop off at their pits half a lap earlier than Mayfield. He wound up coming in fourth. Down in the Lone Star State, Mayfield was one of the biggest contenders at Fort Worth's Texas 500. But a sudden blowout halfway through the race took him out of the pack of leaders. The Texas 500 saw Mayfield finish a dismal 23rd.

After an exhausting series of weekly races, the Pocono 500 was the next stop on the circuit. The tricky, triangular course at Pocono International Raceway would be an ideal arena for a face-off between driving aces Gordon and Mayfield.

Even though he hadn't yet come in first, Mayfield could claim four 1998 top-10 finishes, earning more points than any other driver. Having gotten his chance at the stocks because of his mechanical ability, Mayfield drove with a cool, deliberate style. As much as anything, Mayfield's driving style accounted for his current Winston Cup lead. Going into the June Pocono 500, Mayfield said he counted himself lucky to be leading Gordon by 26 points in the standings. Mayfield praised his crew, especially chief Paul Andrews, for keeping his car race-worthy. Andrews already had a 1992 national championship under his belt.

Racing against Mayfield at Pocono was the usual collection of NASCAR veterans, rookies, and superstar drivers. The top contender was the flashy and successful Jeff Gordon. Even younger than Jeremy by a couple of years, Gordon was the darling of many newcomers to the Winston Cup scene. Gordon was the product of a wealthy racing syndicate, Hendrick Motorsports.

Mayfield, on the other hand, was a pure car guy. A regular working fellow who could not only race cars but build them as well. He had come up the hard way, working in a variety of car shops. When his car broke, he was usually the one who had to fix it.

During the qualifying runs, the first and second pole positions at the Pocono 500 were won by Gordon and 42-year-old Rusty Wallace, respectively. (The first pole position is on the inside front row; the second pole position is on the outside of the front row, and is actually the second starting spot.) Getting these coveted pole positions gives the drivers a lead at the beginning of the race. Although rules vary for different races, the first pole is always awarded to the driver who posts the best time in the qualifying trials. Mayfield lined up just behind Gordon and Wallace in third place. The green starting flag dropped, and the drivers hit their accelerators.

Gassed, tuned, primed, and ready, the colorful stocks bolted forward. One after the other they screamed down the long front straightaway at Pocono, shooting into their turns. Averaging well over 100 miles per hour, around and around the stock cars went, lap after lap. The heavyweight racing tires on the cars held the asphalt pavement like black rubber claws. Like the other drivers, Mayfield steered a fine line between success and disaster, racing bumper to bumper at breakneck speeds.

Stock car racing is a very dangerous sport, and men have died competing in it. Few people have the nerves required to race stocks. The quick reflexes and steady temperament needed to drive a powerful stock car successfully are quite rare. The art of NASCAR racing is the ability to make a thousand adjustments in speed and angle, hour after hour. It means knowing your machine and the other machines on the track. Successful auto racing is about always watching the road, searching for openings, avoiding hazards, and being very aware.

Checking his instrument cluster frequently, Mayfield tore around the track. As he pushed forward, a great shout went up from the crowd of 60,000. He knew that eventually he had to win a big race outright. Maybe Pocono would be it. Before he could snatch the lead, however, he had to battle for position with Darrell Waltrip. Waltrip, a three-time Winston Cup champion and Mayfield's boyhood idol, wanted the win as badly as Mayfield. With about 25 laps to go, Waltrip's Monte Carlo sped past the pack to pull alongside Mayfield. The two racers settled into a high-speed duel, first one and then the other taking the lead.

The noise and the fumes of the stock cars hung heavy over the track at Long Pond. As the lap numbers mounted, the drivers fought bitterly for position.

Suddenly a caution flag dropped, informing the field that rain was falling on the track. At that moment, Mayfield realized that he could win his first NASCAR race.

People covered up as drizzling raindrops sprinkled the stands. The warm June afternoon gave way to an early summer shower. Rain soaked the racers, their pit crews, and the eager, cheering spectators. Then, on the 180th lap a red flag dropped, halting the action for more than an hour.

Restarting after a rain delay is never easy. The rules say everybody has to remain in the same order. Mayfield would have to keep his concentration or he would lose again.

"I knew . . . I had the car that could win the race," Mayfield said. "I was already thinking about Victory Lane . . . and had to regain my focus."

He regained it just in time. When the rain

Streaking down the track at 185.9 miles per hour in a qualifying run, Mayfield's Ford Taurus crosses the finish line at the Texas Motor Speedway at Fort Worth. His phenomenal speed won him the best starting position for the Texas 500.

Mayfield and fellow racer Jeff Gordon (at right) are fierce competitors when they race. Off the track, however, they share experiences. Here, Gordon shows Mayfield how his car handled a turn in a practice session.

stopped, the drivers piled back into their cars. As well as Gordon and Waltrip, top NASCAR veterans Dale Jarrett and Mark Martin were also competing for the lead against Mayfield. They knew just as well as Mayfield how to turn a rain delay to their advantage. When the race resumed, Mayfield stayed firmly in contention. Pouring on the speed, he kept his nimble Taurus within striking distance of first place. As the cars neared the finish, Mayfield raced wheel to wheel with Gordon. Just behind the two leaders was Waltrip, a cagey veteran who was still a force to be reckoned with. Strapped inside his car, Mayfield saw little but the flash and blur of the other racers. At each screaming turn, Mayfield guided his Taurus stock car over the slick asphalt, constantly jockeying for position.

Right beside him, rival Jeff Gordon piloted his Number 24 DuPont Chevy at a blistering pace. Mayfield and Gordon had been rivals for a couple of years now. At this stage in their careers, Gordon had the definite edge. He had won the Pocono 500 two years in a row. As the winner of 32 NASCAR races, Gordon had quickly risen to become one of the top drivers on the Winston Cup circuit. To beat a driver like Gordon, Mayfield had to give it his very best.

Tearing around the turns and running flat out on the long straightaway, the competing drivers went at each other with fierce determination. The 750-horsepower engines in their 3,400-pound vehicles reached the very limit of their performance. All Mayfield needed to do now was concentrate.

Time and time again, Mayfield held off charges from Gordon and Waltrip. A tiny opening in the pack finally gave Mayfield the opportunity he had been seeking all day long. He stormed ahead at the last instant to claim the victory.

Mayfield's win over Gordon was narrow even for a NASCAR competition. He had beat his rival by .341 of a second. However close the victory, winning the Pocono 500 meant everything to Mayfield and his team.

"This is my lifetime dream," Mayfield said, from his special spot in Victory Lane. "I wanted to beat the best and that's what I did."

Sixth-place finisher Darrell Waltrip had only flattering things to say about Mayfield. "Jeremy is a good boy and I'm really happy for him," Waltrip said. "I doubt that is the last time he wins one of these races. Now that he has his first the next victories will come a bit easier for him."

A RACER
FROM THE START

Folks in the small towns of the South are famous for their interest in stock-car auto racing. Most histories of the sport trace its origins to the dirt roads and fields of Virginia, Georgia, and the Carolinas during the 1930s. In those days, illegal liquor runners built fast cars to carry gallons of moonshine from backcountry stills to taverns in the cities.

On the outside, the liquor cars looked like normal, everyday automobiles. On the inside, they were completely different. They were equipped with heavy-duty reinforcement and much more powerful engines. The cars boasted stronger suspensions, linkages, and gearboxes.

Jeremy Allen Mayfield was born into this southern auto-racing tradition on May 27, 1969, in the small Ohio River city of Owensboro, Kentucky. Both his father, Terry Allen Mayfield, and his mother, Judy Allen Gordon, enjoyed racing automobiles and just about anything else on wheels. Before Jeremy

Born and raised in the Ohio River city of Owensboro, Kentucky, young Jeremy was part of the stock-car racing tradition of the South. As a youngster, he worked on cars, thought about cars, talked about cars, and dreamed of becoming a winning race car driver.

As a teenager, Jeremy began racing go-karts in his hometown. These competitions helped give him the experience and skills he needed to eventually graduate to stock cars and enter the major races.

went to high school, he was already a fanatic about auto racing, including go-karts, stock cars, late models, funny cars, drags, trucks, and sprints. (Sprints are typically run on dirt tracks and have a boxlike attachment fitted to the roof for stability.)

Jeremy's uncle and father gave him his first taste of racing, and he liked it right from the start. He later described his feelings: "As I can remember, all I have ever wanted to do is drive race cars and to be a Winston Cup driver." Jeremy showed a single-minded fascination for stock cars that has never left him. Racing was the most important thing in Jeremy's life when he was a teenager. He felt an intense passion for sharp, fast automobiles. In his daydreams, the young enthusiast always pictured himself as the winner of the big race.

"When I dreamed about it, I always saw myself in Victory Lane," he said. "That's one of the neat things about being a kid. You know, of those million or so races I ran in my dreams, I won every danged one of them. A couple of finishes were pretty close but not a whole lot of them."

In 1982, at age 13, Jeremy started racing go-karts in local competitions in and around Owensboro. The local go-kart competitions soon occupied more and more of Jeremy's time. The races looked so exciting that Jeremy's mother, Judy, decided that she wanted to give go-kart racing a try. Ever the helpful son, Jeremy gave Judy a few racing pointers. He told her not to let anyone try to pass her down low. Getting passed down low on a track means being passed on the inside, or lower, part of a banked track.

At the next competition, Jeremy found himself racing against his own mom on the go-kart track. When he attempted to pass his mom down low, she swerved to block his pass. The two collided and their go-karts flipped over. Luckily, they suffered only minor injuries. Later on, Judy also drove on the Kentucky Motor Speedway for a season, in the same competitions as her son.

At the county high school, Jeremy joined a group of boys who worked on cars and spent hours talking and thinking about them. After school they tinkered with any car they could get their hands on, taking it apart and putting it back together. The boys checked for faults in the electrical systems and spotted the cause of oil leaks. They replaced points and plugs. After shining and polishing chrome, they stood back to admire their handiwork. Over and over they revved automobile engines until they were satisfied with the tuning. Often they discussed which cars were best and what kind of car they would own when they were old enough to buy one.

Fortunately for car-crazy youngsters like Jeremy Mayfield, information about souping up autos is available. In the late 1940s the National Association for Sports Car Auto Racing was born. It grew from a few late-night racers who met on deserted roads to sanctioned competitions staged on special banked tracks.

During the 1950s and 1960s, new speedways appeared that resembled miniature superhighways. Two of the biggest and fastest were Daytona in Florida and Talladega in Alabama. Stock-car speed records in excess of 200 miles per hour have been clocked in qualifying races at these amazing tracks.

At Christmastime, Jeremy could always look forward to receiving racing-related gifts such as slot-car sets and radio-controlled, gas-powered model cars. For his birthdays, Jeremy got car tools from his parents, including such items as a timing light, socket sets, and a torque wrench.

As Jeremy grew older, sports-car auto racing was spreading like wildfire across the nation. In the early 1970s, the sport had won millions of followers. They flocked to speedways to see stars like Bobby Issac, Cale Yarborough, Bobby and Donnie Allison, and the incomparable Richard Petty.

The first network television broadcast of the Daytona 500 in 1979 ended with Richard Petty taking the checkered flag. What everyone remembered afterward, however, was the slugfest between Donnie Allison and Cale Yarborough after they deliberately crashed into each other going past the third-turn wall. The two former race leaders exchanged blows while the TV crew ran the closing credits.

President Ronald Reagan also gave motor-sports a big boost when he personally met with Richard Petty after his 200th career victory in the 1984 Daytona Firecracker 400.

The biggest Owensboro racing star during Jeremy's youth was Darrell Waltrip. Jeremy was one of Waltrip's biggest fans, and the young hopeful consciously modeled himself after Waltrip, paying careful attention to Waltrip's career and racing style.

"When I was growing up I always looked up to Darrell," Jeremy told NASCAR Online. "I guess the first time I talked to him was on Eli Gold's show and he was totally supportive. . . . Darrell Waltrip said he was handing over the torch. . . . When you hear that from Darrell Waltrip . . . that's definitely a confidence booster and something I'm very proud of."

While his high-school friends were playing basketball or partying, Jeremy spent long hours working on his car. Despite being out of step with some of the other kids, Jeremy persisted in his dream of becoming a race car driver. He was serious about what he wanted to do and worked diligently at it.

"All I heard was 'You need to be doing something else, you're wasting your time,'" Jeremy said. "[E]verybody thinks you've got to go to

Three-time Winston Cup winner Darrell Waltrip, who also grew up racing in Owensboro, was Jeremy's boyhood hero. Here Waltrip rejoices with his wife, Stevie, after winning the Western 500 and capturing the Winston Cup championship in 1985.

college or play basketball, or go to work at a factory. That made me more determined. I had so much desire anyway, but they gave me the determination to really want to do it."

Jeremy hungered to learn all he could about automobile racing, and by 1985, when he reached driving age, he knew that there are as many types and classes in auto racing as there are vehicles to run on the road. Jeremy's fascination with racing extended to everything from go-karts and late models to sprints and NASCAR-certified machines. "I knew I loved being in something with an engine that had pedals you worked with your feet and could make run fast," Mayfield said. "It gave me such a feeling."

Once he caught the racing bug, Jeremy moved up through the motorsports ranks as fast as he could. The main barriers to his ambitions were the age limits at the various tracks. Soon, however, Mayfield was behind the wheel of street stocks, and then he graduated to late-model stocks. These lower-circuit races were conducted at NASCAR Winston Cup racing tracks in places like Nashville and Whiteville, Tennessee.

Knowing that his chances of succeeding in racing were slim if he remained in Owensboro, Jeremy resolved to leave home when he was old enough to get out on his own. At the age of 19, Jeremy Mayfield left home and moved to Nashville, the city that seemed like the right place to begin. Arriving in Music City with little more than hope and a dream, Jeremy set out to make his mark in the world of NASCAR racing.

ARCA ROOKIE
OF THE YEAR

Upon landing in Nashville, Jeremy Mayfield began hunting for a job. He was determined to do something with cars, to work on them and maybe get a chance to drive. Jeremy figured the short-track Automobile Racing Club of America (ARCA) races, at the Nashville Motor Raceway, as the course was then named, promised the surest route to success.

To support himself, Mayfield planned to take any kind of car job in Nashville he could find. He didn't have much money and couldn't afford to be too choosy. Fortunately, his mechanical skills came to his rescue. He talked his way into a job as a fabricator in the shop of Earl Sadler, a race car owner. A lot of sheet-metal work, called "fabricating," goes into the construction of racing cars. As a fabricator, or "panel beater," Mayfield helped build new race cars, piece by piece. As each car is built, mechanics and panel beaters must put them together, and the panels must fit perfectly.

Mayfield's mechanical skills landed him jobs in auto shops like this one. At the same time, he also got the chance to compete in racing's junior circuit. Within three years, his winning racing style had brought him the 1993 Rookie of the Year title.

Mayfield learned many of his driving skills from his work as a "panel beater" on race cars. He put his experience to good use when he began his racing career at the Nashville Motor Raceway on the junior stock-car circuit.

Beginning his racing career as a panel beater, Jeremy helped put many stock cars together with his own hands, getting to know every part, joint, bolt, seam, and gasket. He did what people always do to complicated devices to understand them and how they work: He took them apart and put them back together again.

Race cars are complex machines. To be race-worthy, special "stock" automobiles are constructed to withstand the rigors of 500- and 600-mile races. When he started out in racing, Mayfield did everything from change tires to refit, overhaul, and customize interiors. Besides fabricating, he ran electrical wiring, checked instrument clusters, attached fenders, pounded out dents, and installed powerful racing engines.

In 1990, Mayfield began racing at the Nashville Motor Raceway. He competed in the late-model division of the ARCA races, a series of events sanctioned as a junior circuit for lower-division stock car drivers, which are below Winston Cup standards. Mayfield saw a chance to get ahead as a driver in these lower-division events. Within a short time, Jeremy Mayfield was standing the ARCA series on its head.

From 1990 to 1992, Mayfield had three ARCA poles, two wins, 10 top-five finishes, and 14 top-10 finishes. His success at Nashville won him the admiration of the professional driving world. Following the 1992 season, the young driver was named the runner-up for the ARCA STP-Prestone Rookie of the Year title.

To win the Rookie of the Year title in 1993, however, Mayfield had to run his best. He did so in fine style, practically setting the series on fire. By the end of his final ARCA season, Mayfield had captured the hearts of ARCA racing fans. He did it by pulling down eight top-five ARCA finishes and 10 top-10 finishes.

As he neared the end of his ARCA career, Jeremy Mayfield proved again and again that he had the ability to move up through the ranks of professional driving. The next logical step was to somehow get into the highest ranks, the Winston Cup series. When Mayfield was awarded the ARCA Rookie of the Year title in 1993, it only confirmed what many fans already knew: Jeremy Mayfield was a rising star.

Winning the 1993 ARCA crown gave Mayfield the recognition he needed to jump to the next level of racing. Later that same year, Mayfield finally got a shot at Winston Cup racing when Earl Sadler agreed to let him run one race for his team late in the 1993 NASCAR season. His first Winston Cup race would be the Mello Yello 500 on October 10, 1993, at the Charlotte Motor Speedway in North Carolina.

Starting the race in the 30th position, just ahead of Kyle Petty, Mayfield finished in the 29th spot. He drove his own car, a Ford Thunderbird Supercoupe, and won a $4,830 share of the purse. It was a small beginning, but he had both started and finished a Winston Cup race.

The winner of the 1993 Mello Yello 500 was former welder Ernie Irvan. The racing press called Irvan a blue-collar-style driver who, like Mayfield, came up through motorsports the hard way.

Whatever the outcome, at last Mayfield had felt the thrill of action in a Winston Cup certified race. He was eager to make sure that it would not be his last. Many young drivers often make poor choices and take risks that end in crashes or brushes with the wall. At 100 to 200 miles per hour, even grazing the concrete wall lightly can be ruinous. Instead of going out like a hotshot, Mayfield drove steady and safe. He soon had a reputation for being the kind of driver who took good care of his car.

"It's very important not to wreck in this series," Mayfield said. "When I came to the Winston Cup, I noticed that owners didn't hire drivers who wrecked race cars. If you try to push it above its limits, you are not going to be successful in this business."

When he began his racing career, Mayfield was totally familiar with race-car engines as well as every other part of a car. Knowing how cars worked was a great advantage in gaining success on the track.

Another major dream came true in early 1994 when Mayfield won the right to compete in the annual Daytona 500 race. Starting in the 40th position, Jeremy had scratched his way up to 30th by the end of the race. It was a pretty decent showing for a raw newcomer to stock racing's grandest event.

Daytona and Talladega are the two ultra-high-speed tracks on the Winston Cup circuit. Because the tracks run so fast, the cars feature carburetor restrictor plates. Carburetor restrictors are special engine devices that hold down power. They are required by NASCAR officials as a safety measure on the high-speed tracks. To win at restrictor-plate auto racing, a driver must occasionally "draft" with another driver. This means following close behind the other car to bolster momentum and reduce wind resistance for both cars. Drafting is just about the only way to move up in the pack when the race cars are hobbled with restrictor plates.

Part of Mayfield's success at the 1994 Daytona can be credited to the fact that he kept learning all he could about racing lore. He listened carefully to older, more experienced drivers when they gave him advice. Mayfield has always kept his ears open for tidbits of information from former NASCAR drivers.

One racing giant who liked Mayfield's attitude in that respect was Buddy Baker. During his Winston Cup career, Baker had the reputation for coming up big at the superspeedway tracks. His NASCAR victories at Talladega in the mid-1970s are still the stuff of legend in the South. Today, Baker is an announcer for televised NASCAR races on cable-channel broadcasts of the Nashville Network.

"Just riding along with a young man like Jeremy Mayfield . . . talking about drafting and the things that go on, I found he's not one of those kids who think they know everything," Baker said. "He listens very closely to what you say, and believe me, he's going to be a star in this division for a long time."

As a young driver-fabricator, Mayfield was constantly reminded that he had to be cool behind the wheel. He knew stock cars are expensive to build and expensive to maintain. Winners are aggressive but not careless with their machines. "I don't think I've lost that

mentality," Mayfield said right after winning his first big race at Pocono. He commented that striving to keep his performance consistent was the main reason for his success.

"You want to run good every week," he said. "The other guys who are right there in the points right now—Rusty, Gordon, Dale Jarrett, Mark Martin, Terry Labonte—those are guys who run well every week. They don't win every week but they are in the hunt every week. If you are in the hunt every week, you'll win your share of races. We'll win our share too as long as we maintain the consistency thing."

High temperatures on a track make for slick conditions. A worker uses a hose to cool down a turn at the Charlotte Motor Speedway, the site of Mayfield's first Winston Cup race.

FLASHES OF
BRILLIANCE

As 1993 turned into 1994, Jeremy Mayfield continued his transition to the Winston Cup series. In early 1994, he drove four races for Earl Sadler. The expenses involved in running Winston Cup races are extremely high, and Sadler was searching for a full-time sponsor to back the Ford Thunderbird that Mayfield was driving.

Most of racing's cost is in the equipment. Like other NASCAR machines, Mayfield's vehicle can be described as a "stock" in name only. Currently, just about the only stock parts left in NASCAR racers are the nose, the roof, the rear-deck lid, and the bumpers. However, the exterior profile of these customized, high-performance vehicles continues to copy ordinary sedans.

Later in 1994, Mayfield hooked up with T. W. Taylor, a race car owner from Virginia, for another four rides. Jeremy qualified in unheralded cars, making do with what he had. Then he got a big break

The road to the Winston Cup series was filled with flashes of brilliance and setbacks for a determined Jeremy Mayfield. Here hanging behind Jeff Gordon, Mayfield holds onto the number-two spot at the Indianapolis Motor Speedway in 1998.

when he took a job with Cale Yarborough's racing outfit. "Cale Yarborough took a chance on me, something I'll always appreciate," Jeremy said. "I must have sounded like Tom Cruise in *Days of Thunder* when I asked him for the job. 'Please just give me a chance.'"

Still, Jeremy worked every day in the race shop, which is uncommon for drivers to do. While working for Yarborough, Jeremy even served for a time as his own main fabricator. "That was experience I wouldn't trade for anything," Mayfield said. "I learned a lot about Winston Cup cars, the kind of education I wouldn't have gotten any other way." He went right on working in the shop even when he became a full-time driver for Yarborough.

"When I wrecked a car, I was the one who had to fix it," Jeremy commented. Serving as his own mechanic taught Mayfield not to drive recklessly on the track, to preserve his equipment, and to squeeze the most out of it.

Mayfield ran the final 12 races of the 1994 Winston Cup season with Yarborough's racing team. Signing on with Yarborough not only provided him with a much better car but showed almost immediately that Jeremy had the gumption it takes to compete at the highest level of stock car racing. Unfortunately, his flashes of brilliance were overshadowed by poor performances in many cases. During the 20 races Mayfield ran in 1994, he demonstrated that he had a lot to learn about winning on the Winston Cup driving circuit.

At the 1994 Pontiac Excitement 400 on March 6 in Richmond, Virginia, Mayfield took the 18th starting spot. He experienced a setback, however, when he finished 27th. The April

17 First Union 400 at the North Wilkesboro Speedway in North Carolina saw him come in 30th. A similar letdown occurred on May 1 when Mayfield crashed on the 110th lap of the Winston Select 500.

Life in the fast lane got a little better on May 29 at the 1994 Coca-Cola 600 at Charlotte, the longest race in NASCAR. Mayfield brought his car in 21st out of 43 starting drivers. Jeff Gordon won the pole award and the race, finishing almost four seconds ahead of runner-up Rusty Wallace.

Through June and July, Mayfield completed his races in the middle of the pack, never faring better than 21st in any of his outings. A typical race in 1994 was his showing at the Miller Genuine Draft 400 in Brooklyn, Michigan. He came in 25th out of a 42-car field, the next to last of the drivers who actually finished the race. A return to Daytona the following month saw him finish 30th at the annual Firecracker 400 on July 2.

Mayfield's car died at the Diehard 500 at Talladega on July 24 when a wheel bearing took him out on the 140th lap. At least he wasn't the only driver to suffer mechanical troubles. Dale Earnhardt and Jeff Gordon both lost their engines in the same race, and Rusty Wallace went out with a burned piston after running only eight laps. Then at the Miller Genuine Draft 400 in Richmond on September 10, Mayfield got in a wild smashup. Luckily, he came away unhurt from that scary wreck at the Virginia State Fairgrounds.

Returning to the Charlotte Motor Speedway, the site of his first Winston Cup race, on October 9, Mayfield came in 20th at the Mello

Yello 500, nine places ahead of his 1993 finish. This time it was Dale Jarrett, not Ernie Irvan, who rode away with the victory.

Mayfield's best race of 1994 was a 19th-place finish at the AC-Delco 500 on October 23 at Rockingham's North Carolina Motor Speedway, a race that was basically on a par with the rest of his rookie season. His final race of 1994 was the Slick-50 500K in Phoenix, Arizona, where he notched a 20th-place finish.

Looking back, Mayfield could say he had a fairly decent year for a guy who had little more than one season under his belt. He managed a 26th-place average in the 20 races that he ran, collecting 1,673 Winston Cup points and taking 37th place overall in the standings. The overwhelming winner that year was Dale Earnhardt, who amassed 4,694 Winston Cup points, 444 points ahead of Mark Martin at number two.

Better yet, in each of his races that year, Mayfield gained experience and savvy, the kind that only comes from competing in a Winston Cup race. When the season ended in November, Mayfield was vastly improved from where he had been at the start.

In the 1995 Winston Cup season, Mayfield was once again driving a Ford and was now sponsored by RCA Direct Satellite Systems. Hurtling along in the Daytona 500 opener, he blew his engine on the 155th lap, coming in 29th in a 42-car field. He did a little better at the North Carolina Motor Speedway the following week, climbing from a 34th starting spot to finish 18th in the GM Goodwrench 500.

The Rockingham showing was Mayfield's best so far, superior to any of his 1994 races. Things got even rosier on March 5 when he

moved up one more slot, coming in 17th at the Pontiac Excitement 400. Another cause for joy appeared at Talladega on April 30. Mayfield fought his way up from a 33rd starting spot to finish 14th at the Winston Select 500. It seemed like a sign of more good performances to come. In race after race, Mayfield was making better adjustments and showing more confidence. All the while he was learning, learning, learning.

On July 16, Mayfield turned in a truly outstanding race, finishing 8th at the Miller Genuine Draft 500. Mayfield handled the tricky triangular track at the Pocono International Speedway with the skill of a veteran driver,

Mayfield experienced first hand the hazards of Winston Cup racing when his number 98 was caught in a three-car smashup in the Miller Genuine Draft 400 at the Richmond International Raceway in 1995.

Mayfield talks with one of his crewmen about a practice run at the Charlotte Motor Speedway. Throughout his career, Mayfield has never lost his love of and enthusiasm for racing, nor his desire to be at the top of his profession.

clawing his way through the pack from a 38th starting spot to finally crack the top 10.

A month later, in Michigan, Mayfield easily ran the D-Oval two-mile track at the International Speedway to finish 12th. He was disappointed, however, not to finish in the top 10 because his qualifying time had earned him a number nine starting spot.

Then, on August 25, Mayfield crashed again at Tennessee's Bristol International Raceway in the Goody's 500. The wreck took him out on the 382nd lap of the half-mile track. It was a bitter disappointment and a particularly painful loss because he had led the race early on, moving up from 30th in the pack.

Mayfield came back strong at Rockingham on

October 22, placing 11th in the AC-Delco 400. But his best race of the 1995 season remained the one at Long Pond, where he had finished in the eighth spot on July 16.

The people who know NASCAR racing best are the ones who were the most impressed by Mayfield's solid accomplishments in 1995. He never really had the best equipment or the best crew in any of his races, although what he did have was solid across the board. The driving championship that year went to a driver who could boast the best of everything.

That driver was Jeff Gordon, who won the 1995 NASCAR Winston Cup championship over Dale Earnhardt by a razor-thin 34 points, 4,614 to 4,580. In stock car racing, victory generally goes to the people who have the most advantages. Mayfield did not have the best. But driving to the best of his ability, he moved up in the point standings from 37th in 1994 to 31st in 1995.

Despite his disadvantages, Mayfield was determined to reach the level at which he could someday compete on even terms with the Jeff Gordons and Dale Earnhardts of the NASCAR world. To achieve that kind of success, Mayfield knew he would have to move ahead.

Building on the strong season he had in 1995, he improved his performance once again in 1996. Mayfield won his first pole position in July of 1996, clocking a sizzling 193.370 miles per hour at the 2.66-mile Talladega Superspeedway. Getting the pole position makes a driver a heavy favorite in any auto race. Winning is a lot easier if you start in the front rather than the middle or tail end of the pack. Mayfield ran his Ford in 30 Winston Cup races in 1996, he

It was Michael Kranefuss, talking here with Mayfield, who gave a big boost to Jeremy's Winston Cup career. Kranefuss has high praise for his driver's abilities. "He is easygoing off the track and a hardnosed competitor on it," says Kranefuss. "This is the type of guy you think of when you think of NASCAR."

scored two top-five finishes, two top-10 finishes, and earned almost $600,000 in cash winnings. He also moved up even higher in the points standings, from 31st to 26th.

Throughout 1995 and until September of 1996, Jeremy Mayfield had stayed with Cale Yarborough as driver and fabricator. Then in September, late in the 1996 racing season, he got a big break when an unusual agreement was struck with John Andretti of the Michael Kranefuss-Carl Haas team. Andretti went to Yarborough's team in exchange for Mayfield. The drivers essentially traded rides, finishing out the last nine races of the 1996 season with their new teams.

Michael Kranefuss offered Mayfield the opportunity to progress to a higher level of Winston Cup racing. "Everybody worked hard and worked together and we just kept getting better," Jeremy said. "Michael Kranefuss gave me a chance to move to the next level."

Mayfield's willingness to work hard and concentrate on the performance of his car became a hallmark of his career. As he explained his feelings: "I just want to race. I want to be in the race car. I love wearing Mobil 1 on my chest and running around in the car. I like looking at it, working on it, talking about it and anything else you can do with it. Anytime I can climb inside and go, that's what I want to do."

Mayfield hoped the 1997 NASCAR season would allow him to do more of what he wanted to do. Thanks to the team change, the 1997 season meant driving for a topflight team and getting behind the wheel of a truly superior car. Mayfield looked forward to making 1997 his breakthrough year in Winston Cup racing.

ALWAYS IN
THE HUNT

In December of 1996, the Kranefuss-Haas racing team hired Paul Andrews as Mayfield's crew chief. The addition of Andrews brought leadership skills and an enviable record of success to a team that sorely needed them. At 40 years old, Andrews was only one of six active crew chiefs to have won a NASCAR Winston Cup championship.

Earlier, during the 1992 season, Andrews had used his organizational talents to guide Alan Kulwicki to the Winston Cup crown. When Kulwicki died in a plane crash, Andrews kept the team going with three different drivers until it was purchased by Geoff Bodine for the 1994 season. A calm, easy-going man, Andrews is widely admired by the racing press for his insightful comments and tremendous knowledge.

The 1997 Daytona 500 on February 16 was a crucial first test for the new combination of driver, team, and crew chief. At the end of the race, Mayfield's

---

Mayfield and crew chief Paul Andrews (left) became a winning combination as they entered the 1997 Winston Cup season. An experienced and talented crew chief, Andrews kept his team "in the hunt," as he expressed it, in every race but one.

41

Ford came in a satisfying 6th place, a major achievement for the reorganized team. The next race was one of the toughest tests in NASCAR racing—the TranSouth 400 at Darlington, South Carolina.

Going into the month of March, Mayfield talked to the press about the unusual egg-shaped track at Darlington. He pointed out how important it was to respect the 1.366-mile course. "The first time I raced at Darlington, I spent a lot of time asking veteran drivers how to get around the place," Mayfield said. "What did I need to do to be successful at Darlington?"

One of the drivers Mayfield turned to for advice was his boyhood hero Darrell Waltrip. Asking Waltrip about Darlington showed how sincere Mayfield was about wanting to learn.

"Darrell Waltrip probably gave me the best advice," Mayfield said. "He told me to respect Darlington and she'll respect you. I've never forgotten that. . . . The guys who can really feel a race car—guys like Darrell or Earnhardt—are the ones who have been really successful there."

During the qualifying runs at Darlington, Jeremy sped around the course at 168.78 miles per hour. In the race, he was determined to follow Waltrip's advice. By respecting the track, he came in 17th. Mayfield's 1997 finish at Darlington was the best showing he had ever posted at the treacherous raceway.

Three April races in 1997 revealed the unpredictable nature of the grueling week-to-week grind that is Winston Cup racing. At the April 6 Interstate Batteries 500 at Fort Worth's Texas Motor Speedway, Mayfield experienced some handling problems to finish a terrible

32nd. Then, one week later, at the Food City 500 in Bristol, Tennessee, he scored a top-10 romp, coming in ninth out of the 43-car field. He did even better on April 20 at the Martinsville Speedway Goody's 500 in Virginia, nabbing a seventh-place finish.

The month of June smiled on Mayfield when he took fourth place at Dover Downs, Delaware, in the Miller 500. Ricky Rudd's Tide car came in first in that race, and nobody except Jeff Gordon shed a tear when the early favorite—Gordon himself—came in a paltry 26th, earning only 90 Winston Cup points.

In the heat of July 1997, the combination of chief Paul Andrews and driver Jeremy Mayfield was really beginning to click. Everybody in NASCAR knows that a solid driver-crew chief relationship is a key to winning. Thanks to the skill of Andrews and the hard work of the Kranefuss-Haas racing team, Mayfield completed 2,900 of 2,905 laps in his last 10 races, second only to Mark Martin's 2,904.

"Paul Andrews is the best crew chief in racing as far as I am concerned," Mayfield said in praise of his crew chief. He also explained how they had achieved such accomplishments when, before the Jiffy Lube 300 at the New Hampshire International Speedway, he noted that "Paul and I have been communicating pretty well. That communication is going to be really important to a good run at New Hampshire."

Looking at the New Hampshire race, Andrews said the flat, one-mile oval track presented a tough challenge to all of the drivers. Because of the lack of banking, they could not depend as much on the handling of their car or the power of their engines.

"Jeremy is really smooth," Andrews said. "He drives smart. He doesn't have the experience a Bodine or a Kulwicki did right now, but he does have the intelligence and patience to do it and do it well."

Despite their good communication, Mayfield, Andrews, and the whole team finished a disappointing 17th at the Jiffy Lube 300. But the very next week Mayfield roared back with a ninth-place finish in the Pennsylvania 500.

Mayfield proved that his Pennsylvania showing was no accident on August 2 by placing fifth in the Brickyard 400 at the Indianapolis Motor Speedway. The Brick is one of the richest races in NASCAR. Mayfield carried home an astounding $142,445 as his share of the prize money.

A pair of late 1997 races forced Mayfield out of the top 10 that year. At the DieHard 500 at Talladega on October 12, five cars spun out of control in wrecks. Mayfield finished running, but came in 26th, barely avoiding a disaster.

Mayfield later said, "I'm not sure what started that deal. . . . But it was one heckuva wreck. I was doing everything I could to miss it, but I got caught up in a cloud of dust and felt the car starting to lift. . . . Then I felt a Whooomp! . . . There was nothing any of us could do. There was nowhere to go and nowhere to hide."

At the Dura Lube 500 in Phoenix on November 2, Mayfield worked his Kmart Ford up from 37th to 19th, but that was not quite enough to keep him from falling out of the top 10. Nevertheless, as the 1997 NASCAR Winston Cup season drew to a close, Mayfield had good reason to be proud. He had logged 15 finishes in the top 20 during the first 20 races, including a string of nine races where he came in best at fourth and worst at 17th. However, the late-season slump dumped him from eighth to a final 13th overall in the point standings.

"We took off and had a really good first half last season," Mayfield said. "In the second half, we beat ourselves."

The 1997 season saw Mayfield make a huge leap in the NASCAR Winston Cup standings, however. He jumped from 26th in 1996 to finish at 13th in 1997. He just barely missed a top-10 ranking by 29 points. Racing consistently throughout most of the season had vaulted Mayfield into the Winston Cup elite.

And yet, an outright victory in any one of the races still eluded him. Mayfield wanted to win a race to get the monkey off his back. Without taking that drive down Victory Lane, Mayfield still carried the status of "junior" driver. He could not yet claim to be a full-fledged member of the club. "Right now, I am probably as hungry to win a race as anybody out there," he said.

During the 1997 off-season, Mayfield suddenly found himself joined with Rusty Wallace on the newly formed Penske-Kranefuss racing team, which came together right after Christmas when Roger Penske bought out Carl Haas to become partners with Michael Kranefuss. Penske is the millionaire head of a large truck rental and transportation services company. Among his many enterprises, he operates auto-service shops at more than 700 Kmart locations around the country.

In addition to Penske's financial muscle, the team received a boost when Penske-Kranefuss chose to form a multicar team rather than start a second one especially for Mayfield.

Initially, Rusty Wallace didn't want a teammate. Among NASCAR veterans, there is often resistance to the idea of drivers in the same race belonging to a "team." Although multidriver teams are not new to NASCAR, the belief exists that owner pressures force the drivers to help each other out in what really should be an "every driver for himself" sport.

However, as a result of their pairing, the two teammates noticed a decided improvement in their Winston Cup racing results. The philosophy of the Penske-Kranefuss team is to always seek a 1-2 finish, no matter what the race. As Wallace put it: "We're both working hard to win. Our driving styles are virtually identical, and we're making each other better. Roger wants us racing each other for the championship at the end of the season."

Going into the 1998 Winston Cup season, racing insiders couldn't see how 1997 champion Jeff Gordon or 1996 champion Terry Labonte could be beaten. After all, these Hendrick Motorsports two top drivers had supplied their sponsor with 22 wins and 18 pole positions in 62 races.

After being winless in 110 starts, Mayfield confronted the biggest challenge of his career. The 1998 NASCAR season promised to be the toughest test he had ever faced. He was determined to do well, not just for himself but also for his new team. And when Jeremy grabbed the Winston Cup points lead during the early part of the 1998 season, the racing press began to call him an "overnight sensation." As a five-year veteran of Winston Cup racing, he was unimpressed by the media attention but pleased with the points lead.

Other drivers were far less pleased with Mayfield's success. During the Goodwrench Service Plus 400 at the North Carolina Speedway in late February, Mayfield tangled with Dale Earnhardt, grazing Earnhardt's black number 3 Chevy. The vengeful Earnhardt then tagged Mayfield in the rear on the third turn, nearly causing him to crash.

Mayfield said of the incident with Earnhardt: "He's just mad because he had a bad day. He won last week, came back this week and didn't run good at all. . . . I'm sure he was frustrated."

As teammates, veteran Rusty Wallace (left) and rising star Mayfield worked well together, sharing information and discussing strategies for winning. Despite Wallace's initial reluctance to drive with Mayfield, he soon began treating Jeremy like a younger brother.

But late in May, Mayfield too had reason to be frustrated when Jeff Gordon won the Coca-Cola 600, bumping him and teammate Wallace to second and third places in the points race.

The 1998 Winston Cup season soured for Mayfield after he lost the lead in points to a resurgent Jeff Gordon. His standout victory in the June Pocono 500 was the last time he would lead the 1998 points race. He came in 18th in California at the Sears Point Raceway after that. Then he entered a stretch of five races where he failed to score any top-10 finishes.

By October, Mayfield had slipped steadily down to sixth place in the driver standings. Going into the UAW-GM Quality 500 at the Charlotte Motor Speedway, Mayfield trailed Gordon by 784 points. As was the case in 1997, his performances lacked consistency. To compete with the likes of Jeff Gordon and Dale Earnhardt, Mayfield would have to dig deeper and work harder than ever before.

Looking on the bright side, Mayfield saw what happened in 1998 as a necessary step in his development. He gained a lot of experience from being in different situations that were unfamiliar to him, such as a stint in Japan. On November 22 Mayfield raced at the NASCAR Thunder Special Motegi, a nonpoints event at a track northeast of Tokyo. Mayfield secured his third career pole by smoothly handling the 1.5-mile course in just over 35 seconds, averaging 158.50 mile per hour during the qualifying run. He pushed Jeff Gordon to second place.

Getting into the spirit of the Motegi competition, Mayfield dyed his hair white. The new color did not seem to have any winning effect, however. Mike Skinner won the race, edging

out Jeff Gordon's Chevy. Mayfield came in a close third.

Mayfield's third-place finish in Japan was not what he wanted, but he felt good about 1998. The Penske-Kranefuss team and its star driver learned some hard lessons about points racing during the course of the season. They also got a pretty good feel for what it would take to win a NASCAR championship.

Now the goal was clear: The team wanted to push Mayfield right to the summit of Winston Cup racing.

Mayfield had reason to smile for photographers at the Thunder Special Motegi in Japan. He had just won a qualifying lap to beat out rival Jeff Gordon for the pole position.

WHEN DREAMS
COME TRUE

The Daytona 500 race is the official start of the NASCAR season. At the 1999 Daytona, Mayfield's teammate, Rusty Wallace, emerged as one of the early favorites, along with Mark Martin, Bobby Labonte, Ken Schrader, and rookie Tony Stewart. The day before the race, Mayfield had a second-place finish in the Gatorade 125 qualifier, which earned him a row-three start in the biggest race of the year.

Expert opinion was divided regarding the likely winner of the 1999 Daytona. One of the favorites at the 1999 Daytona had to be the veteran Dale Earnhardt. When his black number 3 Chevy crossed the finish line first at Daytona in 1998, it was the only time Earnhardt had ever won the big one. He sorely wanted to repeat the feat in 1999. His long experience and aggressiveness made him impossible to dismiss. Jeff Gordon also could not be counted out. Gordon had won the pole position for

Jeremy Mayfield takes the lead at New Hampshire International Speedway in July 1998. As the Winston Cup points leader, he was on his way to making his racing dreams come true.

Drafting in a race gives momentum but is a risky maneuver. To study the effects of drafting, the Penske-Kranefuss team tests the cars of Mayfield and Wallace at a wind tunnel.

Daytona on the strength of his qualifying race and on his status as the defending Winston Cup champion.

Beforehand, Gordon had expressed his concern that drafting, not speed, would be the biggest factor in the race. "If you don't play the draft right, it doesn't matter how much speed you have," Gordon explained.

Drafting at Daytona means trying to maintain momentum in the race. It is extremely risky to follow immediately behind another car at almost 200 miles per hour, but it must be done to plow a path through the furious wind resistance generated at such speeds. Drafting allows tandem drivers to coast by cars that are working alone because they have less momentum.

Drivers find it especially important to be patient and use the draft wisely at Daytona because it is one of two races where NASCAR requires carburetor restrictor plates. Restrictor plates hold the horsepower of the cars down to the 400–450 level. This tends to mean that the pack will be more bunched up. Effective drafting can be used to move ahead of the pack and avoid wrecks and pileups.

Jeremy Mayfield and Rusty Wallace told the press before Daytona that they planned to make drafting work for them as much as they could. In 17 years of NASCAR driving, Wallace had never won at Daytona. "But last year, somehow, we were together most of the day," Wallace said, "and man, did that help."

Mayfield added: "We're going to try to work together the same way we did last year. I hope we can draft right to the end and one of us wins and the other finishes second. But somehow, it always winds up being every man for himself."

Mayfield's challenge loomed no less large than that facing Rusty Wallace. During the early going of the 1998 racing season, Mayfield had experienced a dream come true. He led the standings for a time and won his first Winston Cup race at the Pocono 500. In race earnings, Mayfield had joined the exclusive "Million Dollar Club" in 1996. He moved close to the $3 million mark in 1998.

A few weeks before the start of the 1999 season, Mayfield described his hopes for the coming year to the cable television program *Inside Nascar:* "We'd like to win three to five races, finish in the top three in points and get two or three pole positions. We'd be lucky to do that." When the 1999 Winston Cup season got underway, Mayfield was considered one of the top challengers to superstar driver Jeff Gordon.

Every year Winston Cup drivers hope to make Daytona their first victory on the circuit. Mayfield spoke humbly of his appreciation for being able to participate in grand racing events like the 500. "I'm not the only one on this team but I came up the hard way," Mayfield said. "I did things the hard way, wanting to get to where I am now with this race team and to where I was Sunday at Pocono."

Reflecting on the struggle he endured to become a NASCAR driver, Mayfield expressed gratitude for the help he had received from owners and former drivers. "I had a lot of people helping me along the way but I worked hard and did whatever I had to do to get there," Mayfield said. "[Earl Sadler]. . . helped me move along in my career. From there then I went with a guy named T. W. Taylor out of Virginia."

When the 1999 Daytona race got rolling, Mayfield worked his way up from row three to lead the race briefly before taking a pit stop. On the 135th lap, a brutal collision wiped out a dozen cars in the field, costing the race leaders Dale Jarrett, Mark Martin, Tony Stewart, and nine others a chance at victory.

A caution flag came out again when a late wreck slowed the field. Most of the race leaders, including Gordon and Earnhardt, took the opportunity to gas up and have fresh tires put on their cars. Neither Mayfield nor Wallace

A practice run at the Charlotte Motor Speedway leaves Mayfield wiping the sweat from his face. He is probably the most determined and hard working young driver on the NASCAR circuit.

chose to do so, a decision many Daytona observers questioned. Both drivers elected to stay on the track. Crew chief Paul Andrews said he thought that Mayfield had his best chance to win if he skipped a stop.

The decision was a mistake. Mayfield cut a tire on lap 194, just after he had eased into fourth place. He had to stop, and the pit crew got him back out on the track as quickly as they could. But the pit stop gave Jeff Gordon the chance to sneak into the lead, and for the rest of the race he blocked a charging Dale Earnhardt to claim the victory. Mayfield finished the 1999 Daytona a disappointing 20th.

Things looked up the following week at Rockingham, when racers took on the North Carolina Speedway in the Dura Lube Big K 400. Mayfield called Rockingham the place where the NASCAR season really begins.

"Every year you see guys who have a great Daytona 500, and then you couldn't find them on a milk carton the rest of the season," he said. "The Daytona 500 is important, but it doesn't make or break your season. It's a long, long year and every single race is crucial."

Mayfield's crystal ball was pretty clear at Rockingham. The two Daytona 1-2 finishers, Jeff Gordon and Dale Earnhardt, fell out of the Dura Lube 400 with mechanical problems. Mayfield finished a respectable eighth in the February 21 race, a few seconds behind winner Mark Martin. When the race was over, Mayfield had moved up to third place in the points standings, a tribute to his steady, careful driving style. All during the race, he had stayed in position to win, never falling below eighth in the running.

From Rockingham the Winston Cup circuit moved west to Las Vegas, and after that to California, New York, Texas, and a host of other stops on the 34-race 1999 schedule.

Despite the hectic schedule, Jeremy Mayfield finds time to relax, enjoying free time in the team car-hauler. If he gets hungry, he likes to sit down in front of a bowl of fresh carrots, dipping them in dressing. Before he goes out on a NASCAR race track, Jeremy always eats a peanut-butter sandwich, and during the

season, he consumes a lot of pasta.

Once in a while Mayfield goes back to Owensboro to visit family and friends. He did just that on January 27, 1998, to receive the Excellence in Sports award from Owensboro's mayor. When he is in town, he usually stops at Moonlite Bar-B-Que, a favorite hangout of his. He still knows lots of folks back home and in Tennessee, where driver Josh Harris runs Mayfield's number 82 late-model car at the Nashville Speedway.

Mayfield cheerfully does his share of the promotional work that goes along with being a part of NASCAR racing. It's a fan-friendly sport, and he makes guest appearances at many stops on and off the circuit. An example is the visit Mayfield paid to the Augusta, Maine, Civic

As one of the top drivers in the Winston Cup series, Mayfield often appears to promote the sport he loves being part of. Here, holding the microphone, he and fellow drivers hold a conference with reporters at the Talladega Superspeedway. From left are Jeff Gordon, Jeff Burton, Dale Jarrett, and Dale Earnhardt.

Center to greet fans attending the annual Northeast Motorsports Expo on January 9, 1999.

The three-day showcase featured exhibits representing a wide variety of motorsports entertainment. The show included stock cars, drags, go-karts, truck and tractor pulls, motorcycles, off-road vehicles, and ice racers. Always a gracious guest, Mayfield signed autographs and showed fans the Penske-Kranefuss Racing Mobil 1 Ford Taurus he wheels around NASCAR tracks.

Mayfield is proud of the success he has earned in his sport. From the season opening race in Daytona to the final race at the Atlanta Motor Speedway, Mayfield was just one of two drivers to be 10th or higher in the Winston Cup standings throughout the entire 33-race 1998 schedule.

At home in Cornelius, North Carolina, Mayfield loves spending time with his wife, Christina, and their two cats, Cobi and Butch. Whenever he gets the chance, Mayfield golfs or listens to country music. He is a fan of singer-songwriter Garth Brooks, singer LeAnn Rimes, John Michael Montgomery, and others.

Mayfield is an easygoing man away from the racing scene and counts the Sylvester Stallone movie *Rocky* as his favorite film of all time. He also likes Clint Eastwood pictures and actress Heather Locklear in TV shows like *Melrose Place*.

Fans of racing collectibles should have no trouble finding Mayfield mementos. Die-cast models of his racing cars are available at sports shops nationwide, and his rookie trading card, number 107, in the 1994 Traks Premium set, shot up in value after his breakthrough 1997 season.

Another card company, Press Pass Racing, issued a 1999 set with not one but eight different Mayfield cards. He appears four times in the regular set and four times in the insert cards, including a special "Oil Can" insert that celebrates his car-shop origins. Fans of the NASCAR racing scene agree that Mayfield is an exciting new personality.

After finally winning a race in 1998 and joining the top-10 Winston Cup drivers, Mayfield's ambitions for his career started to soar. Despite his poor showing at the 1999 Daytona 500, he refused to look back.

"Our goals are pretty high," Mayfield said. "We're not cocky but we've pretty well decided that 'the best' is all we want to be. . . . Last year, we were hoping to finish in the top 10 and win a race and a pole. This year we're looking at the top. We want the championship. Why would your goal be to finish second in anything?"

Jeremy Mayfield is one of the hot young guns leading NASCAR into the 21st century. As such, at the end of every race Mayfield expects to take that drive down Victory Lane.

CHRONOLOGY

1969   Born on May 27 in Owensboro, Kentucky.

1982   Begins racing go-karts in his hometown.

1987   Wins Kentucky Motor Speedway Sportsman class Rookie of the Year and Most Improved Driver awards.

1990   Begins competing at Nashville Motor Raceway in Tennessee.

1993   Runs ARCA Series, winning ARCA Rookie of the Year title; enters his first Winston Cup race on October 10, driving for owner Earl Sadler at the Charlotte Motor Speedway in North Carolina.

1994   Finishes 37th in the Winston Cup point standings.

1995   Finishes 31st in the Winston Cup point standings.

1996   Streaks to first career pole at Talladega, Alabama; joins Kranefuss-Haas Winston Cup team in September; joins exclusive "Million Dollar Club" by the end of the year; finishes 26th in the Winston Cup standings.

1997   Joins up with Rusty Wallace on the newly formed Penske-Kranefuss racing team; finishes 13th in Winston Cup standings.

1998   Wins his first Winston Cup race, the Pocono 500 at Long Pond International Speedway in Pennsylvania; finishes seventh in Winston Cup standings.

1999   Enters Winston Cup season as a top challenger to defending champion Jeff Gordon.

STATISTICS

YEAR	RACES	WINS	TOP 5	TOP 10	WINNINGS
1993	1	0	0	0	4,830
1994	20	0	0	0	226,265
1995	27	0	0	1	436,805
1996	30	0	2	2	592,853
1997	32	0	3	8	1,067,203
1998	33	1	12	16	$2,332,034
CAREER	143	1	17	27	$4,659,990

FURTHER READING

Fleischman, Bill, and Al Pearce. *Inside Sports NASCAR Racing: The Ultimate Fan Guide.* Detroit: Visible Ink, 1998.

Hemphill, Paul. *Wheels: A Season On NASCAR'S Winston Cup Circuit.* New York: Berkely Publishing Group, 1997.

Huff, Richard. *The Insiders Guide to Stock Car Racing.* Chicago: Bonus Books, 1997.

Huff, Richard. *The Making of a Race Car.* Philadelphia: Chelsea House Publishers, 1998.

Moriarty, Frank. *The Encyclopedia of Stock Car Racing.* New York: Metro Books, 1998.

ABOUT THE AUTHOR

Mike Bonner has written about sports figures and sports collectibles for *Sports Collectors Digest, Beckett Vintage Sports, Sports Cards Gazette, Delphi Collectibles Forum, Oregon Sports News,* and *Sports Map* magazine. From 1992 to 1993, Mike wrote a column about the football-card hobby for *Tuff Stuff* magazine. In April of 1993, Mike solved the mystery of the player featured on the fabled 1890s Mayo "Anonymous" football card, a hobby landmark. Mike's 1995 book *Collecting Football Cards, A Complete Guide* is a Krause Publications title and is acknowledged as the most complete work on the subject to date. Mike has also written three other books in the Chelsea House Sports Legends series, on NBA forward Shawn Kemp, major league pitcher Randy Johnson, and NHL hockey star Paul Kariya. A graduate of the University of Oregon, Mike lives in Eugene, Oregon, and is married to the former Carol Kleinheksel. Mike and Carol have one daughter, Karen.

INDEX